FACES
IN THE CITY

OTHER BOOKS BY JAMES KAVANAUGH

A Modern Priest Looks at His Outdated Church
The Birth of God
There Are Men Too Gentle To Live Among Wolves
The Crooked Angel
Between Man and Woman
Will You Be My Friend?

JAMES KAVANAUGH

FACES IN THE CITY

*Photographic Illustrations
by Ron Rubenstein*

A Sunrise Book
E. P. Dutton & Co., Inc.   New York

Library of Congress Catalog Card Number: 73-186926
ISBN: 0-87690-164-X

Printed in the United States of America.

10 9 8 7 6 5 4

To those
    who look close enough to see
        the hurt hidden in anger,
        the fear disguised in arrogance,
        the eloquence locked in silence beyond all words,
To those who love the faces in the city

Faces in the City

In the city there are faces
   Confident or afraid
   Strong or delicate
   Wrinkled or yet unformed.
Faces
   Taut and grim
   Open and alive.
Faces wise with life's experience
Faces bland and empty hiding pain.

Joyous faces living each moment
Desperate faces passing the time.

Beyond the color and the forms are the faces
   Sketches never finished
   Tragedy and triumph fighting for mastery.
Faces changing every day
   Or drawn rigid to remain the same.
Faces taught their worthlessness
   Or resisting judgment with a secret strength.
Faces
   Proud of power or bruised by defeat
   Searching for love or proclaiming its presence
      Looking for an answer sudden and absolute
      Looking for a way out soon and magic
      Or content and joyous to be.
In the city, man is the mystery, not God.

Man's face is in the city
   Prisons to tell of pain and despair
   Hospitals to tell of compassion and indifference
   Schools to tell of concern and neglect
   Homes to tell of hope and defeat

Apartments and theatres, bars and delis
Gardens and garbage, racketeers and lovers.
Man's face is in the city
The mayor is his and the council
The streets are his and the beggar
The slums are his and the bells
The parks are his and the children.

Man is the bus groaning up a hill
The department store and crowds
Smiles and curses from taxis
Silent people worrying about Christmas
Salesmen with big smiles and sweaty palms
Poor men struggling
Trucks blocking traffic
Policemen staring
Men and women dreaming and despairing.
No face is alien
Twisted in horror or carved into beauty
Friendly or suspicious.
Judges only judge themselves.

In the city lies man's hope.

He will live there and love there
and raise his children
He will struggle there and cheat there
and learn to be afraid
He will come there and laugh there
and shed his tears.
In the city lies man's future.
The poor are trapped there
The rich are rewarded there
The lonely are lured there
The lovers are loved there
Man will curse it
Despise it, attack it, abandon it
But he will return
For the city is the face of man.

The city
Once built along the rivers
Now harnessed by freeways and subways
Smothered with traffic and trafficking
Is man.
There is no noise like the city at midday.
There is no silence like the city before dawn.
The oceans will soothe him

The deserts comfort him
The mountains will heal him.
But man will live in the cities
Grow in the cities
Die in the cities
Because the cities are his face.

The city is man
Not as we want him to be
But as he is.
The city is you
The city is me
Our own eyes that stare back
When we look and sometimes see
The faces in the city.

NOTES FROM THE STREET...

Man Does Not Live in the Giant City

Man does not live in the giant city
 But in a town of his own making with narrow boundaries
 To shelter him against the enclosing time,
 In a corner somewhere, or a kitchen
 Where someone cares enough to be peevish,
 In a nesting place with a supermarket where he can cash checks
 And knows the checkout lady by name,
 A special parking place, bakery smells and someone to nod to.
 Familiar faces like halloween masks,
 Assorted friends to keep away the darkness,
 In a town where old men can smell the tar of street repair
 And watch the workmen smooth the new cement
 Or see the children skipping home from school
 And making wings and hoods with their coats.

Man does not live in the giant city
 But in a name like New York
 Where he's never seen a play
 But subways in silence till he finds
 The corner where a dog barks at him in recognition.
 He is not as free as his San Francisco
 Nor as energetic as his Chicago
  As pragmatic as his Detroit or Pittsburgh
  Liberated as his Los Angeles

As elegant as his Boston,
Only as gentle and frightened as the little town he clings to.

Man does not live in the giant city
Its arms are too big to hold him,
Its voice too loud to hear him.
His tears are just as lonely in San Francisco as in Fresno.
The nights can be as empty, the days as dark
As many lonely people shuffling through the park
Till man finds his street, his tree
His patch of sun or snow or gentle grass
His place to rest, his chair, his ancient Mass
Or just a thirsty plant that asks for water
A pet or two, a son or daughter
And memories, and hopes and dreams
To know that at the end of every day
Somewhere in his city is a town where he can stay.

A Stone

Once a little stone
   Was lying in a field
Till someone picked him up
   Polished him
Joined him with other stones
   And made him part of a wall.
He wasn't a stone anymore
   Free to lie in the dust
Until the rain came
   To make him clean again.
He was cemented in a wall
   Surrounded, crowded by other stones.
He was hardly noticed before
   Now everyone saw the wall
Of which he was a part.
   But the wall was in a field
And did nothing, protected nothing
   Led to nothing.
It was only a wall in a field
   Standing alone made by men
Who thought they should use the stone for something.
   And the little stone will remain there
Till the wall falls down

Or someone knocks it down.
Then he will be a stone again
   And get dusty, feel the rain
And the soft feet of children.

Notes from the Street

It is Sunday, I've read the papers, and I leave my room in the city
   To walk among the people of the streets and ghettos
   In search of the neighbors I knew.
   Where's Mr. Markley and his gentle pipe?
   Where's the bus driver who knows me?
   Looking for someone to call me by my special childhood name.

I like the streets, the curio shops and the quiet antiques
   The bars and restaurants, vegetables in front of dirty windows
   Sirens hardly heard, snarled traffic and gawking tourists.
   A toughness here among the poor, dreams dim
   Fewer expectations, life settled down to be lived.
   I am a stranger here, not wanted, awkward. I feel afraid,
   Out of touch. Not really my city. Nor my country.
   Hardly my world. I don't belong. The old ladies do
   Shuffling along with their shopping bags. The old men do
   Letting down their awnings and prying open crates.
   So do the blacks who hate me,
   And the angry browns. And the sullen Chinese.
   Once I thought they only smiled
   Now the young are angry, pushing, glancing, narrow eyes,
   Fuck-you eyes, hate-filled. Not yet ready to be sad or afraid.
   Only angry. Not asking or wondering. Only angry.

I want to go away. Back to a gentler neighborhood so long ago
   Where every frame house had a name
   And every dog and every kid, even every old maid.
   Hamburgers after football practice. No claim check at the cleaners
   Or at the bike shop. Steal cherries from Mr. Pritchard's yard
   Back across the boulevard. Read the sports page again.
   New York lost. San Francisco won. Big deal! Go home. Watch TV.
   Where's home? Little boy laughing. Milk bottles on the porch.
   Hole in the screen door. Friendly bushes. Where's home?
   Angry eyes. My eyes. Fuck somebody. Anybody. Any body.
   Forget for a while.

It is Sunday. I've read the papers, and I leave my room in the city
   To choose up sides in the park or take on winners
   To send my brother home for misbehaving
   To tease the girls I want to touch, to spit water
   To find familiar cracks in the sidewalk
   To walk among the men mumbling on park benches
   And hear the accents I do not understand
   And wonder why the slave is gentler than his master
   And more at peace.
I don't know the language here, blunt and unadorned
   Love your parents, go visit them on Sunday,

Earn what you eat. Tip your hat to the priest.
Take care of the store, save if you can, work till you die.
Sundays off, church for the ladies and kids and the old men.
Washing to do. God understands. Fix a good meal.
Maybe dress up, go out, walk the streets, play with children.
Awkward men throwing footballs in the park.
Never had time to learn. The kids don't care.
The crippled girl on the grass, the mongoloid in the shade.
Keep them at home. God has his reasons.
The black boy playing with the simple girl in the bushes.
He won't hurt her. Nobody's business. Certainly not mine.
Not here on the streets. Niceties gone. The queers can hold hands,
Who gives a damn! They don't swear or hurt anybody.
They're alive. The little bald ones are the most desperate,
Looking glum in the coffee houses. No glummer than me.
I don't know the language here. But neither do the young liberals
With their options held in storage for awhile.
Their accent gives them away, suburban overtones.
Too loud a laugh, too big a heart, too cool.
Anger everywhere among the young.
Fear everywhere among the old.
The writers are middle class. So are the movies.
God! So am I! Too free to serve, to regain my body, to flow.
Awkward, stiff, afraid, lost. Take a vacation. Chase excitement,
Go back to school, try something else, move away,

Marijuana, another woman, maybe two orgasms tonight.
No revolution needed anymore. Take my chains. I paid dearly.
What can I get you? A meal, a glass of beer?
I'll empty the crate, I'll let the awning down.
Smile at me. Please smile at me!

It is Sunday, the paper's read, and I leave my room in the city
    To find a little boy I once knew, to forget time.
    To drift and dream and stumble over curbs, to laugh,
    To pet the pony in Wattle's garage, to walk in Kleinstuck's woods
    Or hide in the climbing trees and wait for pot roast and gravy,
    To play six-man at Delano's without coaches or referees.
So I sit in the coffee house and feel my intensity dissolve
    And watch the radical mark his books with yellow crayon,
    Talking ponderously of society and man, blind to the sun
    Making jeweled patterns on the faces of the poor,
    In love with an idea, orgasms of the head,
    Pursuing, chasing, detachable testicles, don't let it get away.
    An afternoon of dalliance would blow his theories.
    Put him with a laughing girl whose breasts bounce when she runs,
    Too joyful to know what he's talking about—or to care,
    To fondle his lips and search his eyes for sore spots.
    Early acne avenged. Nietzsche and Marx and Mao lose out
    To flower picking and dog watching and rolling in the grass.
    Go away young man I've known so long, too tense and sad

To see the girl who serves your cappuccin' and empties your ashes
Or the old lady who waddles by your window.
You fuck me up looking past me through your ideas.
Liberal myopia weaned too soon like me
Else you might have played the flute or baritone
Or delighted your lover or caressed children or smiled.

It is Sunday, I've read the papers—even the funnies
  And I leave my room in the city
  To tease a dog or steal a caramel at the grocer's
  To mimic Mrs. Henry or swagger like Mr. Sims
  To find the policeman who used to muss my hair
  To shake off death and despair for a while
Among the strangers in the porno movies, parlors for the lonely
  Middle-class girls getting permission, earning their letters,
  Liberated housewives coming of age, taboos traded in,
  Side by side with the lonely old men, chuckling sometimes,
  Satisfied with some stirring in their loins.
  Black bras and giant vaginas, grinning, sighing, groaning, lonely.
  Tattooed men, not much popcorn here, cement floors, shuffling,
  Clothes off, down to business, scalpels out, silence, silence.
  Try it again, merging, hungry mouths everywhere, moist, fluid,
  Sweating, dusty films, flecks of light, popping sounds,
  Lips opening and closing, hair and moisture, hands and holes,

Sighing and dying, action tonight, get her excited,
New techniques, little girls sneaking under sheets,
Skeletons and corpses and silence, everywhere silence,
Empty words, no words, no sounds, silence, everywhere silence.

Go away again, depressed, lonely, empty, death,
   Back on the streets voices, noises, stuffy, sad, silent.
   I think I'll go home. Where's home? They stare at me here.
   I'm not of the streets. Too late to learn. All alone.
   Back to my options. Money in the bank. Multiple choice.
   I'll be back. To the neighborhoods. I'm rooted here too.
   My clothes don't show it. Nor my face. Only my gut.
   Mother hold me. I'm your boy. It's Sunday. Walk in the park.
   Mother hold me. I've read the paper—even the funnies!

There Seems To Be Every Indication

There seems to be every indication,
Given our personal freedoms in this century,
    That a proper book on sex will soon be written.
Not one that simply tells of techniques
    Or hangups, or daring positions,
But one that encompasses the history of sex
    And the discoveries, the breakthroughs
    With proper credit lines.
Thus, for example, what school child realizes that
    The English lathe operator, Isaac Henderson Jones,
    Discovered twelve hundred and seven erogenous zones?
Or who has heard of
    The Frenchman Jean-Paul Currière Rippe
    Who measured the thrust of a rotating hip?
Or did you yourself know that a black man,
    The immortal South African, Gerard Duncan Speers,
    Was the first to make use of the circular mirrors?
And a little closer to home
    That the American publisher, William Adair,
    Was the very first man to print pubic hair?
And isn't there room for a chapter or two
On the bizarre deviations of charismatic leaders
    Like the great naval hero, Washington Lammock,

Who could only perform in a zebra-striped hammock?
Barring sexual backlash and sudden underpopulation,
There seems, indeed, to be every indication
   That a proper book on sex will soon be written.

A Shy Child's Eyes

A shy child's eyes
Look out and say
    "If I come outside,
    "Will you promise not to hurt me?"

The body emerges first
Sliding carefully like a cat
Dragging the eyes behind
    To take the dare
    And dive in cold water
    Or lace up skates with frozen hands
    Or swim across the channel
To please the people who are not respecters of eyes
    Until one day the eyes appear at little slots
    From behind rusty, iron walls
    And look carefully out
    Begging not to be hurt.

City Girl

City girl
  Pursuer of fashions, up on plays,
  Frenetic enough, good at words,
  Reader of magazines, critic of movies,
  Tight around the lips,
  Red wine with beef
  And sex after dinner and the late news.
City girl
  What shall we talk about tonight?
  The effect of LSD on babies?
  Murders in the city—and rapes?
  Did you know that a beggar stabbed three men
  On their way from the ice follies?
  You read it, too?
City girl
  I like it when you drop your guard,
  Your eyes go droopy and soft,
  Your breath sounds helpless,
  Your face prepares for some explosion,
  And touching replaces talking.
  Maybe that's why I hurry you to bed.
City girl
  Your window box looks like a garden now,
  Your fish tank bubbles like a waterfall,

Cars on the street sound like crickets and frogs
And lonely owls in the night.
And I can taste the country on your lips.

They're After Me Again

They're after me again!
It all started when I bought a house
And the insurance companies found out about it
Because my mortgages were suddenly public knowledge
And letters came from all over to tell me that for a fee
They would bet I'd die before the mortgages were paid
And if so they'd appear and leave my house all free and clear.

When I refused to bet my house against my life
The insurance companies gave up on me—
Which kind of hurt—and sold my name
To extension classes and correspondence institutions.
I only had to check a single box and I'd get information
On how to be almost anything. Like this one guy
Who had been a part-time gardener and ended up a stockbroker—
Which is supposed to be a good deal.

Anyway I considered being a lawyer—to fix my own tickets,
Or a CPA—to do my own income tax,
Or I could learn to manage a restaurant and meet lonely women,
Or a hotel and get special rooms for my friends.
I could even be a commercial artist and paint murals in my bathroom
Or a traffic manager and figure out a better way to get downtown
Or I could be a diesel mechanic and take people on my own train
To football homecomings, or maybe fill the cars with kids

Who'd never left the city and make enough money doing this
To call the insurance companies and bet my life against the house.

But with all my dreams I lost the reply card about the time
The scientologists got my address, followed by three missionaries,
Two bishops from the Southwest, four pool salesmen
   And a prepaid burial program.
Then apparently the extension's classes gave my name
To the book and magazine people since it was obvious that
Without a decent job I had a lot of time to read.

Actually I ended up beating these bastards at their own game.
Although I finally subscribed to four magazines and three book clubs
And an encyclopedia on sex which came almost free with the one
On ocean fish, nevertheless I qualified for the bonus
Which gave me ten chances on a grand prize
   To pay off the whole damn mortgage!

Come, Walk the City

Come, walk the city in the late night's silence
    When the bars have closed and the laughing conventioneer,
    Stripped to his shorts, surrenders to the pain lines in his cheeks
    And wonders if his wife can turn him on,
When the virgins are all safely bolted in bed
    Reading novels to discover how life should be lived,
    When the prostitutes gather to talk of health foods
    And the wealthy regular they knew in Florida,
    When the garbage man begins his day in strident disdain
    To gather landfill for future development,
    When the morning papers are bounced from trucks
    Like trussed bodies with a secret story to tell,
    When the city like some aging, weary giant
    Collapses on the pavement to decay and die,
    When the taxis play tag with their golden lights in the night
And deliver the drunks who can't find their cars,
    When the flotsam people crawling from some unrecorded wreck
    Slump in the doorways of deserted stores
    To warm their legs with the evening news,
    When a misty rain falls upon the mystery men
Who shield themselves in the shadows of the night.

Come, walk the city in the late night's silence
    When the buses are heaped together to rest their groaning gears

And the patroling police surprise the lovers in their cars.
When the poor relieve themselves in alleys,
And leave the trees and bushes to the dogs,
When the forgotten men with no more dreams
Wander in their grey garb blending with the night,
When the street lights turn their whiskers to golden stubbles
Of wheat and transform the haze of their eyes into a wistful shine,
When their tattered clothes give them freedom to drift
Into places where policemen carry guns,
And gentle faces made soft and distant by pain too deep
For memory stare at ladies and know that their glances
Will never be returned or will be shuddered at,
When the men free enough to lose their respectability
Approach a stranger for a cigarette or beg for a quarter,
When the men who know they'll always lose
Quit before the struggle begins
And gather soberly to watch the night get cold.

Come, walk the city in the late night's silence
To meet the men with no one to count on,
No one eager for a call, no one to contact on holidays,
No one to love them at all,
Meet the fathers and brothers now unclaimed
Who tell stories of the past and study the eyes of the listener

To see how long the interest lasts.
At night the city is more theirs than anyone's,
Its very curbs their couch, its parks their playground.
They know the secret corners where the morning sun sneaks through
To warm their hands, the secluded spots to sleep and fantasize
And drink cheap wine in paper sacks.
They know the cracks in sidewalks, holes in streets,
The outlines of the buildings, and reflections of the moon.
They can spot a tourist, a detective, a pusher, the moods
And temperament of the police. They hear the sirens
And see the crimes, they stand back from life as spectators,
Unconcerned with wars or investments or rising crime rates.
And when the morning comes and traffic roars
And the successful men and women pour from buses, file along
The streets, rush to fill their offices and skyscrapers,
They stand along the curbs and watch and wonder,
And know, indeed, that in the night, when the city is silent,
The meek and lonely vagrants take possession of the earth.

*THE CITY IS
MAN'S
MADNESS*

The City Is Man's Madness

The city is man's madness
   A tower of Babel to defy the gods of time and death,
   A woman sneaking glances in store windows
   Wondering about sagging breasts and wrinkles in her neck,
   A man pulling in his stomach, brushing hair over his baldness,
   The young laughing and crying without having to try,
   The old living and dying without knowing why,
   People scurrying, running, hurrying,
   People desperate, anxious, worrying.
      People mounted in clusters.
The city is man's madness
   A perverted seed of Adam spilled at the head of rivers,
   A dream fashioned by the side of man hidden in shadows,
   The master plan of a sadist never satisfied
      Who tears down buildings to build bigger ones,
   Tragedy time, when brothers hate brothers
      To cling to their jobs,
   A giant colony of cannibal ants rushing in all directions
      Because the word is out a beetle died.
So man has built his cities
   Raised the price of land till each building
      Leans on every other,
   Built until the sky is beyond reach or recognition
   And in every building, screened from the stars,
      There's a king, faceless and nameless,

And in every office too
   A king
In every crevice as well
   A king fighting for his kingdom,
    Battling like a beast for a piece of ground
     Big enough to be buried on.

Within These Latter Days

Within these latter days and strangely fearful times
   Of rising stress and weird, apocalyptic signs
When mortars flash like lightning East to West
   And prophets crowd the streets to talk of sudden death
When tidal waves and earthquakes threaten frightened men
   And new messiahs call apostles once again
Where once the faithful built cathedrals in their town
   Basilic banks now rise to consecrate the ground.

Rouen, St. Peter's, Notre Dame and ancient Chartres
   Are vanquished now and soon will rot and fall apart
And in their dust will rise a great financial shrine
   Where marble pillars form a monument, divine
With sacred sanctuaries, eternal granite walls,
   With tabernacled vaults and deeply hallowed halls
And sometimes busts of saints who learned their doctrine well
   That only faulty credit dooms a man to hell.

The sacrifice is subtle—blood need never flow
   As long as true believers pay the debts they owe—
No waiting judgment till some final trumpet call,
   The Book of Life's contained in cabinets by the wall,
Confessionals for debtors, sinners must atone,
   And excommunication when the credit's gone.
And soon, I've heard, a vested choir, a European organ,
   With stained glass windows overhead of Astor, Ford and Morgan.

It's
Eye Catching
Time

.t's eye catching time,
The eloquent language of the city
   More honest than most of its words.
I want you
   But if I told you
   You'd probably run away.
So I'll just look
   On streets and subways
   Through car windows
   In supermarkets
   And restaurants
And maybe I'll catch your eye
   And wonder.

Of All the Professions

Of all the professions that are devious and dirty,
Let's say there are perhaps twenty-five or thirty,
I would say that lawyers somehow lead the list
Of professionals who really get me pissed.
The union plumbers often have a greedy way about them
And real estate developers will often double deal;
Car salesmen are thought to be duplicitous and cunning
But lawyers learn to steal.

I've been cheated by mechanics grinding more than valves
And I've learned that doctors practice usury and medicine;
I've been ill advised by brokers who can't advise themselves
And I wish electricians had to take an oath to Edison.
Morticians make additions in the cost of man's demise,
Police and politicians have been known to take a deal,
The labor union tactics seldom come as a surprise
But lawyers learn to steal.

Thus our system leaves its victims in the cold
Whether wife or husband, worker or employer
Because anyone who's wronged is quickly told
"You'd better get a lawyer."

The Building Inspector

It really would be nice to remodel the basement.
   Do it myself—it'll hardly cost a thing.
I'll have a pool table, a party room, murals,
   Maybe a sauna bath and a real wine cellar.
Not that I drink a lot of wine, but it's nice to say
   "And here's my wine cellar." That's class.
I'll get my permit, start digging a bit,
   Get the floor in. Nothing to it. I should what?
Reinforce the foundation? It looks okay to me, inspector.
   Well, of course, I want to do it right.
      You only do it once in your life.

I need a new storm drain, concrete below the mud sill?
   What's a mud sill? And a two-inch vent?
The furnace pipe is too low? Too old?
   Dig four inches deeper? But it's just a party room.
Well, it *would* be inconsiderate of my seven-foot friends.
   Another window? And a fire exit? Of course, inspector.
I want it right. You only do it once in your life.
   Hello, inspector? You can't come till Friday?
But the ready-mix man is here, he charges by the minute
   And the countdown's begun. Could you talk to the plumber
Who's talking to the carpenter

While waiting for the gas man?
It really would be nice to remodel the basement.
Do it myself—it'll hardly cost a thing.
You're damn right
You only do it once in your life.

The Policeman Caught Me Today

The policeman caught me today
   With his big, red, rotating light
When I picked up hitchhikers too far from the curb,
   A boy with a yellow beard, a stringy-haired girl
   And two very happy dogs.
The policeman lectured me today
   With his big, red, rotating face
Pivoting angrily on his big, red, rotating neck.
   I wanted to laugh—since he seemed overdressed
With a big, fat gun in his belt,
   A sawed-off shotgun on his dashboard,
And a club as big as a Little League baseball bat
   Facing a gentle boy and girl and two very happy dogs.

The policeman gave me a ticket today
   Because I endangered lives,
Though the streets were quiet, the traffic thin
   And the sun brighter than the big, red, rotating light.
Then he was off with justice satisfied, secret scars avenged,
   To rummage through backpacks, to apprehend speeders
With the same red, rotating face
   That captured murderers and rapists.

The car was quiet, the happy dogs growled,
 And it made me wonder
What kind of kids
 Would grow up and want to be policemen.

Sometimes I Feel

Sometimes I feel I may have succumbed to the city's ways
Because nothing seems to save me from the way I was,
Which, from mounting evidence and unsolicited advice,
    Seems really terrible
Because it appears that everyone expects to live forever
    Either in this world
    Or in the next
    Or, if at all possible, in both.
It's not that I haven't tried the city's cults.
    I attended the Self-Realization Fellowship—
    Which seems to be a sensible amalgam of East and West
    And perhaps North and South—
    Where our leader reminded us that God
        Does not torture us beyond our endurance—
        Whereas I had never imagined he would torture us at all
        Unless, of course, this was a subtle reference
        To the sermon which was fifty minutes long,
    But I did hold my offering loosely in my right hand
        As I was told.
Later I discovered that the scientologists accept personal checks
        And like to be paid in advance like colleges and dance studios

Since they have developed a program so ethical and integral
That even Freud and Jesus would presumably be on the mailing list.

Even later the evangelists reported for my edification
That God gave His only begotten Son for my salvation—
Which only made me wonder how the Son felt about the gift.
And at a very religious school
A reformed boy told me that Jesus was more powerful than LSD
Which I knew would make the surgeon general very happy,
And a girl with rather stern eyes insisted that sex
Was from the devil which I am ashamed to say
Only made me wonder how devils do it.
And I followed the Hare Krishna parade
Which promised to calm my mind for the rest of my life
Whereas the Mormon missionaries wanted me for two years
Offering me a break on my hospitalization
And two good acres in Utah.
All of which made me feel terribly guilty
When I gave up my quest and went home
And watched a very old movie on TV
And wondered if the stray cat I was feeding regularly
Really gave a damn about me.

It's Friday Night in the City

It's Friday night in the city
   The singles' bars explode to announce the weekend
   For which the week was made.
   Slow down, Monday will never come tonight.
   Find the eyes that look back,
   Start a conversation. Find the words.
   Don't let her drift away. Slow down. It's early.
   Not much of a face, but check the body.
   Rooted, earth mother, something to cling to.
   Find the combination. Make it right.
   Loosen up. Not too heavy. Get another drink.
   Make her laugh—they like to laugh.
   The regulars move easily.
   The frightened talk too much.
   The cabs are spitting out the strangers.
   Big in their own territory.
   It's not too late. Remember that night in Boston?
   Divide and conquer. Which one do you want?
   Touch her arm. Easy, not too fast.
   Move her out. Too noisy to talk. Get some air.
   You're home. It's Friday.
   Monday will never come tonight.

It's Friday night in the city
   The neighborhood bars explode to announce the weekend

For which the week was made.
Familiar faces. Friendly. Refuge.
Time for bowling scores and golf swings.
Time to hear about Harry's divorce.
Dave's got a new story. Tell it again.
Couples laughing, couples talking,
Couples sitting quietly, familiar territory.
Play a game of pool, shake the dice for music.
Buy a drink for the ladies. The usual.
Pockets of people. Someone knows my name.
Al's drunk again. Arguing. Get him a cab.
Tenderness. Understanding. Cut him off.
Funny since he lost his wife.
Where are we? Somewhere. Anywhere.
Kids got the flu. School's too crowded.
Mother died. Sorry to hear it. She wasn't old.
How's the new job? Chance to make some money.
Car broke down again. New baby coming.
Go home. Happy. Laughing. It's Friday.
Monday will never come tonight.

It's Friday night in the city
    The streets explode to announce the weekend
    For which the week was made.
    Restaurants crowded. We have your reservation.

Ladies laughing. Waiters rushing. Nice to see you again.
Another round. We're not in a hurry.
What do you recommend? Lamb's always good here.
Music. Voices. Leave it to Wally. He knows.
French wine's better. House dressing. More butter.
Medium rare. Romaine lettuce. Isn't that Audrey?
Theatres crowded. Get a cab. Row nine. Not bad.
Called a month ago. Dark suits. Capes. Elegant.
Ladies laughing. Ladies talking. Ladies pointing.
Men smiling. Let's get a smoke. Get a program.
Restrooms crowded. Wait in line. Wash your hands.
Tie looks nice. A little paunchy. Getting older.
Let's have a nitecap. Call the sitter.
Kids got the flu. School's too crowded.
Mother died. Sorry to hear it. She wasn't old.
I'll take the check. Write it off.
Go home. Great evening. Laughing. It's Friday.
Monday will never come tonight.

PORTRAITS...

Little Boy

Little boy lost in color and sound
Sucking in the visions of the town
    Laughing on cable cars
    Wandering through crowded stores
Free to see
    To hear
    To be,
Oblivious even to me.
Absorbed enough to stumble,
    To spill his coke
    To forget where he is
    To forget who he is
Too busy to brush his hair.
Too alive to wash his face
Too much himself to talk until he feels like it.
Knowing what he wants and asking for it
Wandering among ten thousand
    Who do not know what they want
    And if they did
    Would be afraid to ask.

A Funny Little Smile

He's got a round, puffy face
    With sad, red-rimmed eyes behind tinted glasses
    His mouth set in a funny little smile
    And he smacks his lips when he sips his martini.
He's an executive and he drives a big car
    And waits for his wife just as long as she wants
    Because he's grown old enough to compromise
    And to know that happiness
    Comes only now and then.
So he's got a round, puffy face,
    With sad, red-rimmed eyes behind tinted glasses
    And his mouth is set in a funny little smile.

A Quiet Girl

A girl waiting for a bus
   On a grey, cold morning,
      The sun still tucked behind buildings,
   Eyes hazy and soft as the air,
   Damp and only half-emerged from sleep,
      Innocent as animal's, as quietly protesting,
The smell of a quilt still on her legs,
   Soft dreams of night still moistening her loins,
   Her coat pulled tight, the wind blowing her hair,
She is silent, almost sullen,
   More beautiful than the night before.
A quiet girl whose face does not frighten me,
A gallant girl, whose body aches a bit,
   Pleading for a little more time in bed
And the bus will come and she will be gone.

A Lonely Lady's Eyes

A lonely lady's eyes looking for love,
Knowing it will never come,
Obvious eyes, longing, hurting,
Too weary for games anymore,
Silent eyes, tired of an empty bed,
No one to touch in the night's stillness,
No odor save her own grown inoffensive,
Not even a shoulder to kiss, or hair to caress.
Who will save her from the afternoon movies?

Even now the eyes grow guarded as I stare,
Afraid of one-night stands,
Sensuality turned mercifully dull,
Hungry, hungry eyes,
Wounded, tender eyes,
Angry, frightened, hopeless eyes,
So many mysteries in a single glance,
So many tears unshed on dark eye sills
With no one left to be wept for.

I Have a Friend Who Never Laughs

I have a friend who never laughs,
  A strange and silent man
  Who speaks to only a few—
    And rarely.
  He follows the fog
  Stands on high hills
  Drifts along the ocean
  Walks among rocks
  And disappears in eerie caves.
Or he wanders along the river
  Where the cold air
  Makes the children shiver.
And when I asked him why he never laughs
He said that nothing was very funny anymore.

Apartment Four Upstairs

Today I wondered about love
   And saw an old couple returning from the market,
  She with her varicose legs
    Like splotches of grape jelly on bread,
  He with his swollen, arthritic knee
    And emphysema wheeze.
They paused at the bottom of shaky, white steps
And grinned when he handed her the grocery bag.
  She went first, painfully, slowly,
  He followed, stiff hands pushing her rump.
And at the top he gently goosed her.
  She shrieked a bit, he coughed,
They laughed and disappeared inside apartment four upstairs.

Politician Time

It's politician time in the city
And candidates gather in old bingo halls,
   Church basements, or dreary lodges
To tell the people of garbage and jails,
   Clean water and no more cavities,
   Sewage tax and buses, ecology and new schools,
   Police chasing prostitutes, police walking streets,
   Building codes and housing plans, jobs and welfare,
   Drug traffic, game rooms for the old, homes for the poor,
And everything for the children.

It's politician time in the city
And philosophers put down their pens
   To see man as he is,
To see promises, programs, yesterday's movies,
   Placards and pamphlets, pictures and slogans,
   Coffee and cookies, cake instead of bread,
   Neighborhood passion, angry voices, heavy accents,
   Screaming ladies, applause, men smoking pipes,
   Fussing babies, delighted children.
   Words and smiles, words and charges,

Words and threats, words and words,
And everything for the children.

It's politician time in the city
When people not really believing in the process
   But not knowing what else to do, gather
To hear them out, ten minutes a man,
   Nice to be here, just want to thank you,
   Where do you stand, what about the record?
   Square-jawed sheriffs, tough ex-cops,
   I've been around, dark blue suits, life in the raw.
   Oily men for mayor, cautious, elegant, smooth lawyers,
   Charming statesmen, even a woman, too cool, too kind,
   Only the biggies make the papers,
   Only the biggies get the funds.
And everything for the children.

It's politician time in the city
And restless people gather on folding chairs,
   Running for coffee, feet shuffling,
To see old councilmen telling jokes, beat the system,
   Twenty years late, they tore my posters down,
   Stand on my record, sit on my ass.
   Young commissioners, smooth and not Jewish anymore,

Only pogroms in the blood, Irishmen with bushy hair,
Good talkers, natural politicians, nice teeth,
Young idealists, old syndicates, labor tells the story,
Blacks and browns turning white from martinis and handshakes,
I'm from the people, I walk the streets, I know the people.
   Who knows the people? What people?
Candidate night, paper on tables, paper on the floor,
   Pictures, placards, programs, words,
And everything for the children.

Somehow

Somehow his friends didn't know it
 Though commuting together each day,
Somehow his face didn't show it
 —The incredible price that he paid.

Promptly he traveled each morning
 After jogging and kissing his wife.
How did it come without warning
 —This pitiable snuffing of life?

Here was a man of the city
 In the prime of production and speed,
Not a pale one to mother and pity,
 —The commuter's commuter, indeed.

Would I could finish the story
 With a bold, cinematic-like flair.
Somehow the end should be gory
 —That he died in a duel in the square.

Would he had challenged commuters
 Or had leaped from the twenty-third floor,
Would he had smashed the computers
 Or left with a great, final roar.

What in his life had unmasked him
   That he lay down his head and just died?
Why when the operator asked him:
   "Please dial nine for outside!"?

I Saw His Face

I saw his face today
   More handsome than most
   Formed in an Arab village
   Laughing in the sweet air of Lebanon.
   Chasing goats in the rocks of Syria
   Or shouting in the muddy water holes of Jordan.
I saw his face on the subway
   Profile of a diplomat
   Black hair stiff as Jericho's palms
   Nose strong as Mount Nebo
   Jaw firm as ancient cedars
   A sullen wisdom about the brow
   Face of a nomadic king, a bedouin seer,
   Patient enough to govern and to understand.
But then I saw his eyes
   Beaten soft and silent into subjection
   A docile camel's eyes that once had lived
   Made submissive and afraid in bondage
   And I wanted to ask
   "How did it happen, my friend?"

The Man at the Corner Cleaners

The man at the corner cleaners committed suicide today.
Some trembling hand made desperate took his life away
    And left a familiar corpse with a hole in its head.
We knew him well.
    ...Well...we knew him
And talked of politics and children
        Graft and football games
Of schools and rising prices
        Police and business schemes.
    We never talked of death.

The man at the corner cleaners committed suicide today.
Business has never been better, or so my neighbors say,
The stories of those who knew him grow longer every day,
The old are hushed and silent as they pass along that way
    And no one mentions death.

Even in Kansas City

Even in Kansas City
  The French lady sings "Malagueña" in Le Bistro
And the conventioneer from Davenport who requested it
  —To the dismay of friends who never heard of it
Or got it mixed up with "Granada"—
  Taps his foot and gives the lady a couple of dollars
  —More for her cleavage than her voice—
  And later asks for "Guantanamera" and "Cuando Caliente el Sol"
Which he remembers from a vacation in Mexico.

I had hoped to hear "The Man from Laramie" or "Back in the Saddle"
  But two-dollar drinks, red velvet drapes,
  A bartender with puffy sleeves, wicker baskets of cold popcorn,
  Assorted nudes in gold frames and a French singer
  With her picture in the lobby under a special light
  Make the man from Davenport realize he's where the action is.
So he got his "Malagueña" and his friends dozed off—
  And Kansas City was as bland and faceless and lonely
As anywhere else.

Serene Old Lady of the Afternoon

Serene old lady of the afternoon
  Shuffling along sidewalks on aching feet,
  Little patches of hair on legs still beautiful,
  Flesh softer now, resting hesitantly on well-traveled bones,
  Sagging gently in submission to what the years have told you.
  Head bowed a bit as if to shrink from harshness,
  A child's eyes, but wiser, more alive, and moist
  In the breeze that blows the city's dust about.
  Grey hair flecked with specks of auburn
  Recalling what was and knowing that it was enough.

Serene old lady of the afternoon
  Pleased with so little now,
  Laughing at TV cartoons, weeping at soap operas,
  Drawn from memories to the theatre of the sidewalks,
  Revived by city sights and children coming home from school,
  By store windows and conversations on the corner,
  Gentle rituals of fish to feed,
  Birds to scold and chatter with, plants to tend,
  A houseful of knick-knack history, a little soup to make,
  Some nice, fresh corn, maybe a pork loin, a tiny one,
  To make the kitchen smell like it used to.

Serene old lady of the afternoon
  I see your sisters angry, embittered, whining, complaining,

Distressed at life's ending, resenting their children,
While somehow you have outwitted death by living,
Somehow moved beyond time and tragedy to wonder,
Until all your wrinkles lead to your eyes and disappear
In some soft and mysterious immortality.

*OF WOMEN
AND MEN...*

Ode to a Relationship

Well, Marge girl, we've done it all
   Remember the yoga sessions—how I straightened out my spine
      Until I stretched my knee ligaments
   And then we went to the sensuality classes
      And you finally had your orgasm, standing up—in line—
      While we were waiting to see the porno movies.
   And then the two months of group sex right after
      We took the classes in learning how to fight
   And we separated our apartment from the kids and started
      Childlike to eat popcorn in bed
      Like the man from the seminar said.
   And we confronted each other and dealt with things
      Whether we wanted to or not
   And we went to the Jesus happening and then the guitar Masses
      And I became a block captain in the twelfth precinct.
   Remember how I learned to play the guitar
      And we sought new answers in the stars
   And I dropped out of the scouts and the rotary
      And we got our ten-speed bikes.
   Then we tried massaging each other in orange flower water
      And tried 21 new positions until your back gave out.
   Then the trip to Europe, and we learned to make our own pottery,
      Grew marijuana in the basement and did that thing on mescaline
      Until the porch swing broke.

Then we moved to the country, Marge, grew our own vegetables,
   Took vitamin E, and learned to fly fish.
Then we got the sauna and you began to read cards
   And brought the guru to stay with us for a month
   Until he choked while braiding his hair.
And I gave up cigarettes, girl, then booze
   And we both got hooked on kumquats.
Then the commune summer, the swingers' party and the extension classes
   And we sold our stocks and invested in real estate
   And stopped seeing your mother, and even mine.
Remember, Marge, remember . . .
   Well now I know what it is, baby.
   It's you, and I'm splitting.
You piss me off!

Your Body

Your body brings back childhood smells
    Fruit jars in a damp cellar
    Bread dough rising near the fire
    The musk of burning leaves
    Tomatoes ripening on the vine
    Cornsilk cut for cigarettes
    Sheets and T-shirts dried in the wind
Your body brings back childhood smells
    Apples turning to cider
    Freshly cut pumpkins
    Mother's winter coat
    Dad's easy chair
    Incense and candles in the old church
    The pantry at grandma's house
Your body brings back childhood smells
    And friends I've known
    And moments when "someday"
    Promised everything.

You're Nothing Special, Silly Man

You're nothing special, silly man
  Save of your own making.
  A fantasy of someone's aching,
Someone who needs you
  Because the nights are long,
  Someone too desperate to be alone,
  Someone to figure you out,
And to make of your trembling an orgasm.

It's not your fault, silly man,
You're a god who makes love from clay.
  It all began with mothers' wombs
    Feeding you alone
    Protecting you alone.
  It all began with mothers' hands
    Holding you alone,
    Loving you alone.
But you will know
  In the eyes that wander
  In the hands that pull away,
You will know
  When your arms are betrayed
  And love is gone,
That you're nothing special, silly man.

Some Angry Man Appeared Last Night

Some angry man appeared last night
   Summoned by the genie of gin,
A stranger, vague, but remembered,
Frightening, fierce, wounded, wounding,
Who trampled on wisdom and gentleness
   Earned in so many battles won,
   Fashioned by so many wounds
   Discovered and healed.

Today the angry man is gone, and in his wake
   Shattered statues, altars overthrown—and shame.
The grinning genie is appeased,
   He proved his point:
Fury still lurks in silent corners
And gentleness must hesitate to claim a victory.

Who Will Love Me in My Madness?

Who will love me in my madness
  When the fearsome mornings come without warning
  In the melancholy of soft rain
  And the dull grey days?
  When I dare not tell you who I am
  Patched together with string
  Fumbling, fearful, lost?

Who will love me in my madness
  When you seek to lean on me
  To glean from me some strength
  That yesterday I seemed to have?
  When I'm sure that I have failed
  And am not strong at all
  And want to run away?

Soon my madness will be gone
  And I will laugh every time I see the sun
But in those mad and fearful times
  Who will love me?

Pretty Girl

Pretty girl playing the games you were taught
Doing what you know you're good at
Still a little girl and no one knows.
You should have been plainer pretty girl
Worried about a crooked nose
Or teeth that wandered.
Glances come too easily your way
Never missed a party, always had a name,
Every day to play the pretty girl game.
Never had to let your daddy go
So you're still a little girl—
And no one knows.

At This Moment

At this moment
    I am all alone.
No heart knows what my heart feels
No lips capture what my lips long to say
No eyes read the message of my face
No ears reassure me that I have been heard.

What do I want you to say?
    Some magic word of love
    To take my sadness away?
I asked too much
    Something no one can give.
Perhaps it is enough to know you care.
    Perhaps enough.

Are You Satisfied?

Are you satisfied my love?
Did I wait long enough
Shake hard enough
Or move slow enough?
Did you come? Or will you?
Shall we try a new position
Or a new partner?

This Really Attractive Girl

I met this really attractive girl
   Like the floating one in the shampoo ad
Who found me as exciting as a sought-after man
   Like maybe an actor or a DJ with his own show
And she really listened while I talked
   A hell of a lot more than I intended to.
And after dinner in her favorite restaurant
   Where she knew the waiters and the "in" wines
And a lot of guys really stared at her
   Which made me, so to speak, very proud,
We really got it on, after I circled the block four times
   Trying to find a parking space and to retain my poise.

And all the time I kept thinking about this woman friend
   Who is no mistress of the manuals
And really no match for this really attractive shampoo girl
   But with whom I laugh a lot and talk only when I want to.
I thought about watching a movie on TV, eating pizza on the floor,
   Picking my feet and spilling my drink as usual, and hearing
"Do you wanna?" And answering "I dunno, do you wanna?"
   Until we fell asleep just holding each other.
All of which led me to believe
   There's a hell of a lot to be said for comfort.

Tonight

Tonight I just want someone to cling to for awhile,
   No words, no analysis, no solutions.
Yesterday I really had it together,
Now there is some weariness beyond all words
   So let me hang on
     For a little mothering or fathering
     Or whatever.
Hold me. Please hold me!
   I'm in another one of those alleys—black and musty,
   Socially unacceptable again.
No questions please. Not even names.
   A cat's not enough. I need you. Not because you're you
   But because you're warm and alive
   And I need you
     Not your mind
     Not your experience
     Not your love.
Just your body. Your arms. You.
     Is that so bad?

Of Women and Men

Women, indeed, have never been paid
The salaries they've long been deserving,
Feminine nerves are unquestionably frayed
By the chauvinist men they've been serving.

Sisters, indeed, have seldom received
The choices and chances of brother,
Feminine hands have but feebly achieved
In the role of a mistress and mother.

Mothers, indeed, have submitted their lives
To the dominance fostered by fathers,
Girls in their teens always longed to be wives
Since their options were molded by others.

Man, it is true, went to work and to war
But consider the freedom he's given—
Males bought the house and purchased the car
Leaving shopping and cleaning to women.

Angels are men and God is a male
Even doctors and lawyers most often,

Men are preferred at Harvard and Yale
And are usually first in the coffin.

Men are retired and women are fired
Only rarely can ladies drive taxis,
Women who hope to be easily hired
Are required to be simple and sexy.

Men have it made, we're gross, overpaid,
We deserved to be quartered in sections,
But ladies be kind and please bear in mind
What it takes to sustain an erection.

THE CITY
LIVES

Who Will Make the City Joyful?

Who will make the city joyful
   Who will wipe away its tears?
Who will fill the streets with gladness
   Who will calm the old folks' fears?
Who will tell the children stories
   Who will make their clear eyes gleam?
Who will keep the men from killing
   Who will give the women dreams?

Maybe twenty thousand minstrels
   Twenty thousand poets' words
Maybe fifty thousand dancers
   Maybe clowns and talking birds
Flowers on all the city's corners
   Trees on all the city streets
Maybe fragrance from the sewers
   Sing-alongs in subway seats.

Maybe buses painted purple
   Maybe no more numbered days
Bells that ring in all the buildings
   Merchants learning how to play
Maybe parks for picnic lunches
   Waterfalls and bubbling streams

Maybe flowers on cold computers—
   Crowning IBM machines.

Maybe plumbers playing trumpets
   Salesmen strumming their guitars
Lawyers nursing tender flowers
   Businessmen exploring stars
Maybe potters, weavers, artists
   Craftsmen, architects who dare,
Maybe muralists and sculptors
   Maybe anyone who cares.

Maybe honest politicians
   Radicals with angry screams
Maybe socialists and Marxists
   Maybe silent men who dream
Maybe shoppers loving beggars
   Gently smiling flower maids
Those who listen to the children
   Those who still enjoy parades.

Who will sit among the flowers
   See the sun and sky above?
Who will make the city joyful

Who will make us laugh and love?
Maybe mothers loving babies
    Maybe gentle eyes that see.
Or beyond the other maybes
    Maybe you and maybe me.

Families To Be Found

In the city
    There are families to be found
    Scattered lavishly around
    In silent places
        To replace the one that's lost
            By death
            Or distance
            Or quarrels never healed
                As happens.

There is a grandmother for those who need one,
        Grey-haired and gentle
        With cakes to bake
        And love left over—never used.
There is a grandfather for those who want one
        Quiet and eccentric
        With gifts to buy
        And stories left over—never used.

In the city
    There is blood-love
        The kind that flows
            When hearts expand.
    There is cross-breeding

And genealogies are mended
Or improved.
There are families to be found.

Doom Prophets Say

Doom prophets say ·
Greedy man will take my world away—
My flowers
My birds
Streams I've fished in
My trees
My ocean
Fields I've wished in.

Doom prophets say
Greedy man will take my life away—
My air
My food
The city sounds and sights
My fog
My bridges
The building shapes at night.

Doom prophets say
That all will pass away.
But I want them to know,
Despite statistics
I don't die easily.

I'm Not Sure

I'm not sure that anyone would understand
    In Scottsdale or Winona,
But there are many days
    When the city is so much mine
That the sounds of traffic
    Are the background stereo which soothes me,
When garbage cans piled in alleys
    And lunch bags littered along the curb
Seem like lovers' clothes, recovered in the morning
    Somewhere between the sofa and the TV.

Sometimes I Realize

Sometimes I realize
    That there are bus drivers who like their jobs
    Black kids who are happy
    Women who enjoy being mothers
    Freeway snarls that give people time to think
    Policemen who can make mistakes and laugh
    Old folks who aren't despondent
    Factory workers who hum all day
    Married couples who are in love
    Girls who aren't afraid to walk at night
    Kids who think school is really fun.
Sometimes I realize
    That there are teachers who enjoy their classes
    Longshoremen who think they're well paid
    Hunters who don't have a masculine hangup
    Children who love their parents
    Rich people who could be poor with dignity
    Girls who don't want bigger breasts
    Men and women who aren't afraid to die
    Doctors who care and don't overcharge
    Politicians who tell the truth.
Sometimes I realize that I am very happy.

I Must Follow Him

Some Gaelic sailor lost at sea
    Still lives inside my limbs.
From time to time he calls to me
    And I must follow him.
I wander from the city's lights
    To walk along the bay,
I hear the creaking, restless ships
    That draw me far away.
I drink my beer in brawling bars
    And scorn the life I lead,
I pause at night to hear the sound
    Of foghorn symphony:
The snorting tubas in the haze,
    The groaning of trombones,
The oboes, flutes, the violins,
    The moaning baritones.
I see the ghostly dancing
    Of the ballerina gulls
And watch the mystic motion
    Of the fog-enshrouded hulls.
I sleep with lusty women
    Who taste of salt and sand
Whose arms are like the groaning waves
    And legs are like the land.
My beard grows free as winter squalls,

My skin like canvas-sails,
I have no time for scholars' words
   But only seamens' tales.

I feel the night upon my face,
   The sun upon my skin,
I taste the salt upon my lips.
   My heart beats hard within,
My hands grow tough, my body lean,
   I take no note of time,
I sleep in clothes I've worn all day
   And smell of sweat and grime.
And I swear that I will not return
   To pallid, somber men
Or lie on sallow-women's sheets
   Or lose my life again.
I will not live by rules of fools
   Where scoundrels say what's fair,
I will not live in city streets
   Where death is in the air.
I will not walk where pale men walk,
   I will not know their pain,

I will not honor God or man
   To live my life in vain.

And when he leaves, this rugged man,
   And I am all alone
I make my way through city streets
   And climb the stairs to home.
My heart is happy once again,
   My chest is strong and free,
I settle down to live my life
   Until he calls to me.
And someday soon, I know full well,
   When pallor chalks my skin
The Gaelic sailor lost at sea
   Who lives inside my limbs
Will once again call out to me
   And I will follow him.
Will once again call out to me
   And I will follow him.

Of
Soft Clothes

I've never worn clothes
    As soft as your breasts
Nor slept on silken sheets
    As gentle as your face.
Maybe if you went away
    I'd care about clothes or sheets
Or the rugs on the floor
    And wonder how I can live
Without a garbage disposal
    On this busy streets with whining wheels
And sirens all night long.

But now I know that
    Joy is where you are
Peace where you live.
    No seascape I've ever seen
Can match that look in your eyes.
You bring the islands to me, the palms and the gulls.
    And when I wake
Amid traffic and garbage trucks and screaming sirens
    I smile.

The City Lives

I came to the city
  Because man is mostly here
  And will always be—
  And presently I choose to be where he is.
Once I thought that beauty
  Was only in the mountains
  Or by the sea
  Or where forests shelter the flowers
But I find beauty here as well
  Confusion grown friendly
  Discord turned to melody
  Swarming bodies to take attention from my own.
I find beauty when
  Hamsters in pet store windows surprise me
    Like giraffes in a jungle clearing,
  City lights from high hills shine like the stars.
  Children lean against No Parking signs to wait for buses
    And still read about Cinderella,
  Lovers laugh and tease in parks
    And seem as carefree and joyful as those by the sea.
Somehow the city is more man than the rest
  Man is not as overpowering and relentless as the ocean
  Not as serene and distant as the mountains
  Not as solemn and silent as forests—

Only sometimes.
Somehow the city is man
   Afraid and dauntless
   Gentle and frenetic
   Hurting and hoping
   Living and dying
   Huddled together and drifting apart
   Leaping from bridges and skipping from school
   Afraid—so afraid
   But laughing often laughing.
Reality is on the faces of the people
   Waiting solemnly for buses
      Silently for elevators
      Patiently in supermarkets
   Waiting shyly in clinics
      Expectantly at movies
      Despairingly in unemployment offices
   Believing it has to be this way
   Almost accepting it
   And laughing often laughing.
Reality is on the faces of the people
   Finding peace amid traffic
      Excitement amid confusion
      Joy amid fear

Finding a lover from a thousand faces
Flowers on a window sill
Fresh bread and silent gardens
Finding antique stores and secret restaurants
Love and children
Hopes and unending dreams.
Man is here
All sides revealed.
Here are the people, the horns, the shuffling feet,
The cabs, the lights, the business beat,
The shouts, the rush, the crowded street.
I need you now. I've found you now.
Death be still. The city lives!

James Kavanaugh on James Kavanaugh

"I am one of the searchers. There are, I believe, millions of us. We are not unhappy, but neither are we really content. We continue to explore life, hoping to uncover its ultimate secret. We continue to explore ourselves, hoping to understand. We are drawn by the ocean. . . . We like forests and mountains, deserts and hidden rivers, and the lonely cities as well. We searchers are ambitious only for life itself, for everything beautiful it can provide. Most of all we want to love and be loved."—*There Are Men Too Gentle To Live Among Wolves* *(1970)*

"Who am I? I am not sure. Once I was predictable. I was educated, trained, loved—not as I was, but as I seemed to be. My role was my safe way of hiding. I was approved, I pleased. Then almost suddenly, I changed. Now I am less sure, more myself. My role has almost disappeared. My roots are not in my church, my job, my city; even my world. They are in me. Friends are not so easy to find—and I dream a lot."—*Will You Be My Friend? (1971)*